D1326484

BEIJING

Richard Platt

Illustrated by Manuela Cappon

KINGFISHER

Beijing

At China's northern edge lies a vast flat plain, bordered by mountains. Icy winds blow in winter, but the summers are stifling. Hostile neighbours threaten from the north. It seems an unlikely place for a city. Yet here, in the 17th century, a glittering, fantastic palace towers over China's capital. At its centre, guarded by high walls, the emperor rules like a god, from a golden throne. The city is Beijing, meaning 'northern capital' in the Chinese language. The walled palace is named the 'Forbidden City'. At this time, it is at the height of its glory.

Beijing is a great city, but it is not the first one to be built here. Before Beijing came Ji, and then Zhongdu, which was followed by Dadu. Each was bigger and better than the city it replaced. The Forbidden City was built in the 15th century CE. Chinese emperors will live here until the 20th century.

RUSSIA

OUTER MONGOLIA (Khalkha)

EASTERN TURKISTAN (Xinjiang)

QINGHAI

TIBET

North America

Europe

Asia

Africa

South America

Australia

BRITISH INDIA (now India)

Bay of Bengal

The Forbidden City will survive wars, fires and revolutions. Its amazing past is the story of China itself. When you read these pages, you will retrace this history and discover how a swampy camp eventually became the world's greatest, grandest palace.

China and its neighbours in the 17th century CE

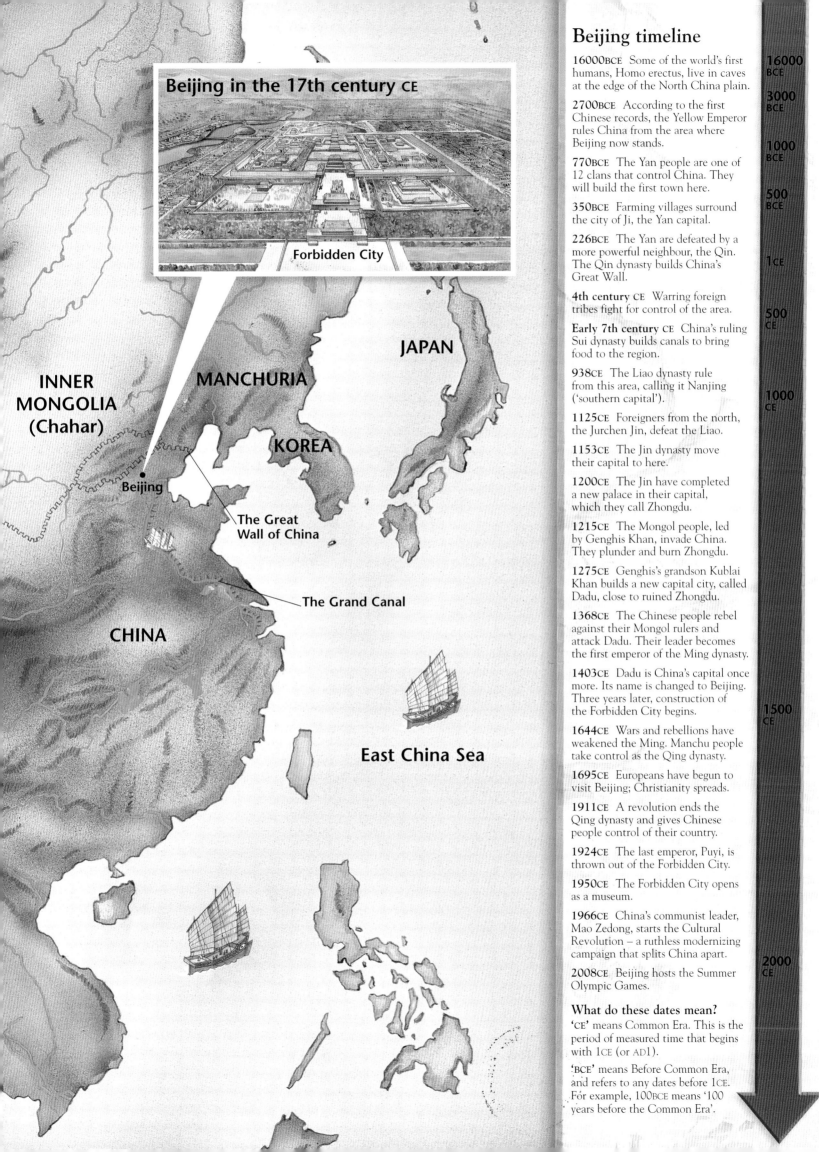

Beijing in the 17th century CE

Forbidden City

INNER
MONGOLIA
(Chahar)

MANCHURIA

JAPAN

KOREA

Beijing

The Great
Wall of China

The Grand Canal

CHINA

East China Sea

Beijing timeline

16000BCE Some of the world's first humans, Homo erectus, live in caves at the edge of the North China plain.

2700BCE According to the first Chinese records, the Yellow Emperor rules China from the area where Beijing now stands.

770BCE The Yan people are one of 12 clans that control China. They will build the first town here.

350BCE Farming villages surround the city of Ji, the Yan capital.

226BCE The Yan are defeated by a more powerful neighbour, the Qin. The Qin dynasty builds China's Great Wall.

4th century CE Warring foreign tribes fight for control of the area.

Early 7th century CE China's ruling Sui dynasty builds canals to bring food to the region.

938CE The Liao dynasty rule from this area, calling it Nanjing ('southern capital').

1125CE Foreigners from the north, the Jurchen Jin, defeat the Liao.

1153CE The Jin dynasty move their capital to here.

1200CE The Jin have completed a new palace in their capital, which they call Zhongdu.

1215CE The Mongol people, led by Genghis Khan, invade China. They plunder and burn Zhongdu.

1275CE Genghis's grandson Kublai Khan builds a new capital city, called Dadu, close to ruined Zhongdu.

1368CE The Chinese people rebel against their Mongol rulers and attack Dadu. Their leader becomes the first emperor of the Ming dynasty.

1403CE Dadu is China's capital once more. Its name is changed to Beijing. Three years later, construction of the Forbidden City begins.

1644CE Wars and rebellions have weakened the Ming. Manchu people take control as the Qing dynasty.

1695CE Europeans have begun to visit Beijing; Christianity spreads.

1911CE A revolution ends the Qing dynasty and gives Chinese people control of their country.

1924CE The last emperor, Puyi, is thrown out of the Forbidden City.

1950CE The Forbidden City opens as a museum.

1966CE China's communist leader, Mao Zedong, starts the Cultural Revolution – a ruthless modernizing campaign that splits China apart.

2008CE Beijing hosts the Summer Olympic Games.

What do these dates mean?

'CE' means Common Era. This is the period of measured time that begins with 1CE (or AD1).

'BCE' means Before Common Era, and refers to any dates before 1CE. For example, 100BCE means '100 years before the Common Era'.

16000
BCE

3000
BCE

1000
BCE

500
BCE

1CE

500
CE

1000
CE

1500
CE

2000
CE

Contents

The book you are about to read follows the history of the city we now know as Beijing. It will show you different palace cities as they are created, expanded, invaded or even destroyed. You will also witness the growth of an amazing and secretive place, the Forbidden City, and trace its story through to the present day.

350BCE   **1200CE**   **1290CE**   **1406CE**

16000BCE

1179CE   **1215CE**   **1368CE**

What does this locator map mean?
As each new city is built, or an older one destroyed, this map shows you the position of these different places in relation to each other. The outline in red shows where you are each time.

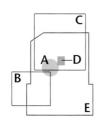

Life in the palace
page 22

The Boxer Rebellion
page 32

Museum city
page 40

European visitors
page 28

A new age
page 36

1480CE   **1695**CE   **1900**CE   **1924**CE   *Today*

1514CE   **1644**CE   **1860**CE   **1919**CE   **1966**CE

Fire!
page 24

Western troops invade
page 30

The Cultural
Revolution
page 38

Fall of the Ming
page 26

The last
emperor
page 34

A marshy home 16000BCE

On a flat, swampy plain, not far from a winding river, a family is hard at work. Beneath a scrubby tree they use the freshly hunted deer to prepare food and clothing. It is a long and messy process, and everyone helps. Skilled hands wielding razor-sharp stone tools neatly separate the skin from the meat and bone. Cooked over a carefully tended fire, the juicy venison will feed this large family for several days. The clothing will last them much longer.

These people are hardy survivors. Their ancestors have lived here for some 300,000 years. They are descended from one of the world's earliest species of people: Homo erectus, or 'upright man'. Living in caves in the hills nearby, these were among the first humans to make stone tools and control fire.

a deer hunter accidentally disturbs an Asian black bear

the climate is warmer and wetter than it is today in this region

hunters can build temporary shelters quickly, from branches and leaves

the family's clothes are made from animal skins, sewn with bone needles

The bones of some of the world's first people, called Peking (Beijing) Man, were found near here.

newly shaped stone blades are as sharp as a modern surgeon's scalpel

pine trees grow
on the hills

hazel and elm trees
on lowlands provide
fuel and materials

hunters must be
fast and cunning to
spear the shy deer

In this era, the marshland people
make early forms of jewellery out of
stones, shells, bones and animal teeth.

hungry hyenas smell meat
and threaten the camp

tools and weapons are made
from stone, wood and bone

hackberry trees
produce a sweet
fruit like a date

The plain-dwellers are highly
skilled at shaping stone tools
by chipping and hammering.

a mother tends
to her infant,
away from
the hunting

The busy family will never know that
the place where they live will become
the centre of one of the most powerful
empires the world has ever known.
In place of mudflats and crude shelters
will grow the vast and beautiful city of
Beijing. And at its very heart, behind
high walls, will lie a magnificent,
secret palace: the Forbidden City.

7

Working the land 350 BCE

Over many thousands of years the Chinese people find better ways to feed themselves. They learn to grow crops and tame animals, which they then use for food. Bronze, and later iron, tools replace their stone blades. By the 4th century BCE a village is thriving on the flat plain. Its people live in thatched huts and tend neat fields nearby. The fields go right up to the walls of Ji, the capital (main city) of the region.

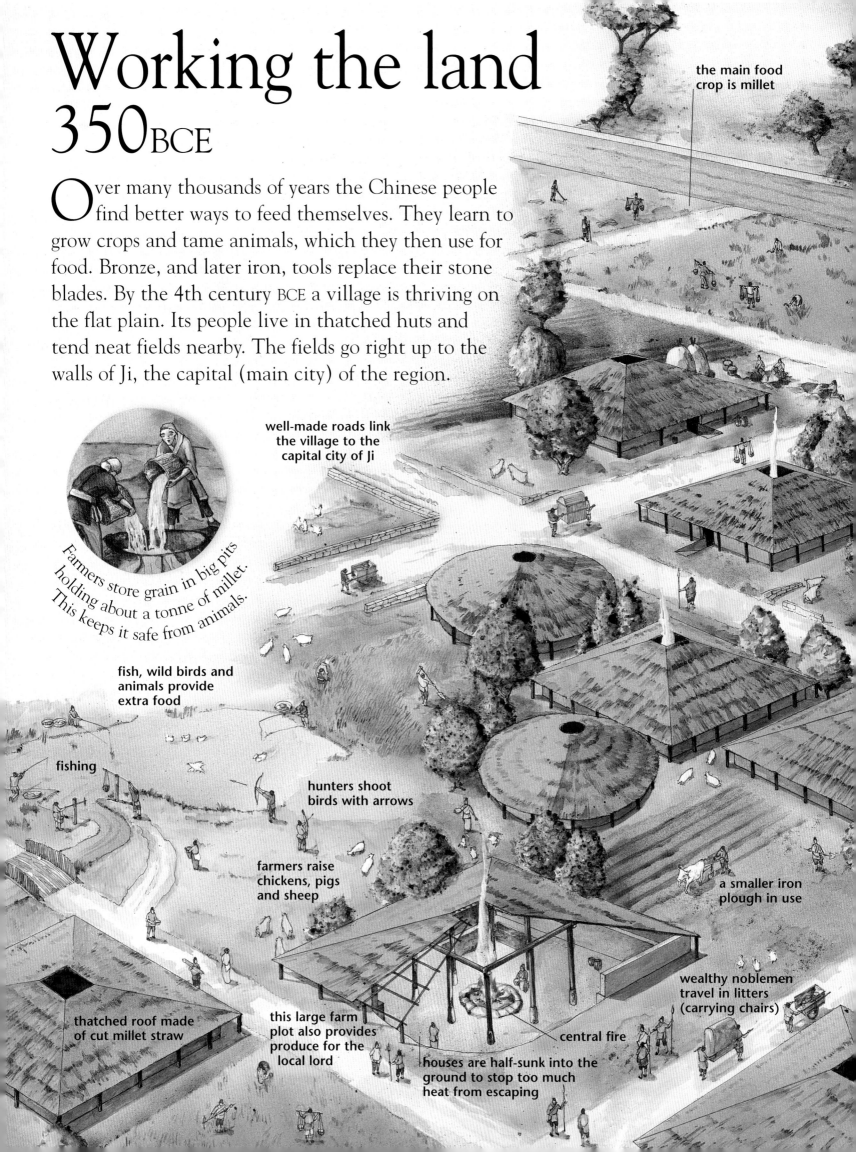

the main food crop is millet

Farmers store grain in big pits holding about a tonne of millet. This keeps it safe from animals.

well-made roads link the village to the capital city of Ji

fish, wild birds and animals provide extra food

fishing

hunters shoot birds with arrows

farmers raise chickens, pigs and sheep

a smaller iron plough in use

wealthy noblemen travel in litters (carrying chairs)

thatched roof made of cut millet straw

this large farm plot also provides produce for the local lord

central fire

houses are half-sunk into the ground to stop too much heat from escaping

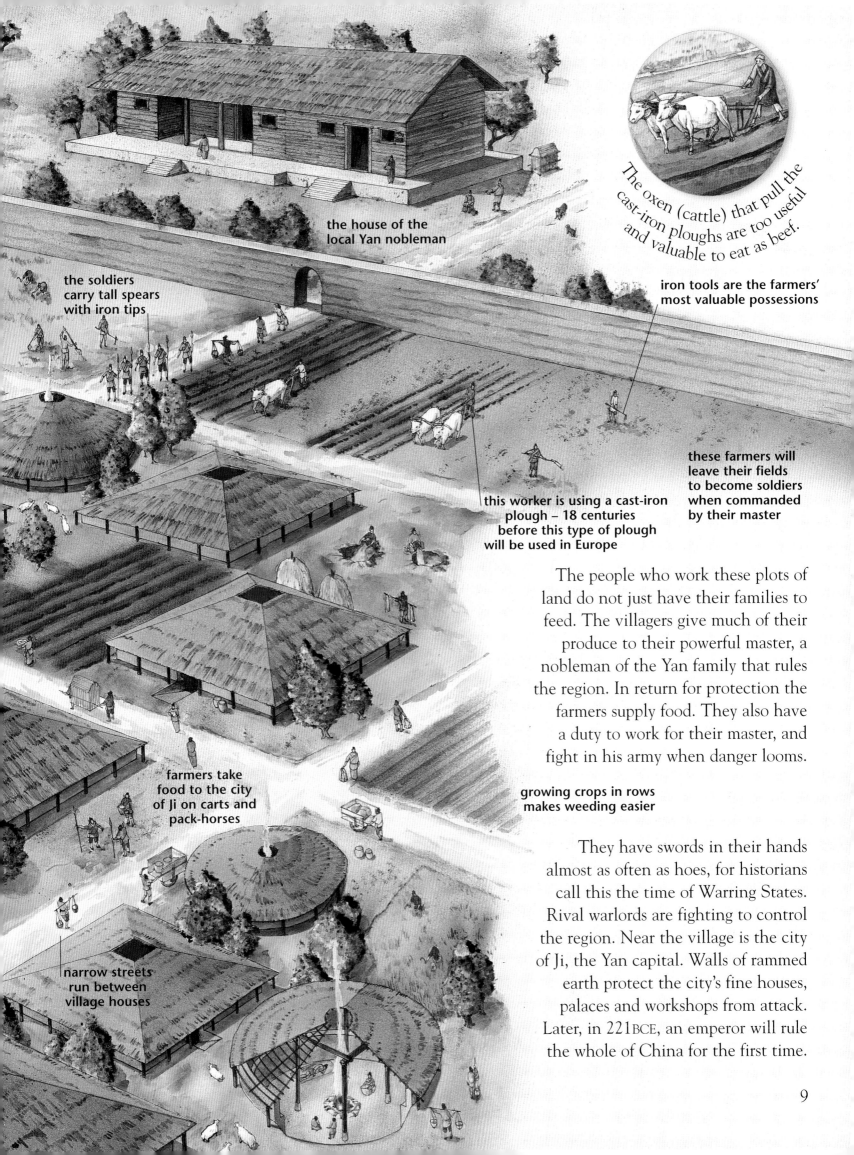

the house of the
local Yan nobleman

The oxen (cattle) that pull the
cast-iron ploughs are too useful
and valuable to eat as beef.

the soldiers
carry tall spears
with iron tips

iron tools are the farmers'
most valuable possessions

this worker is using a cast-iron
plough – 18 centuries
before this type of plough
will be used in Europe

these farmers will
leave their fields
to become soldiers
when commanded
by their master

The people who work these plots of
land do not just have their families to
feed. The villagers give much of their
produce to their powerful master, a
nobleman of the Yan family that rules
the region. In return for protection the
farmers supply food. They also have
a duty to work for their master, and
fight in his army when danger looms.

growing crops in rows
makes weeding easier

farmers take
food to the city
of Ji on carts and
pack-horses

They have swords in their hands
almost as often as hoes, for historians
call this the time of Warring States.
Rival warlords are fighting to control
the region. Near the village is the city
of Ji, the Yan capital. Walls of rammed
earth protect the city's fine houses,
palaces and workshops from attack.
Later, in 221BCE, an emperor will rule
the whole of China for the first time.

narrow streets
run between
village houses

9

Building Zhongdu 1179CE

Fifteen centuries have passed, and the village is so ancient that its origins are forgotten. The community of thatched huts disappeared long ago. Eighty generations of farmers built new homes on the same spot. Each one eventually burned, rotted or crumbled. Smart new wooden homes stand here now, but not for long. The expanding city is about to sweep away the whole village.

For northern China now has a foreign emperor, and he is building a grand new palace capital. The ruler is one of the Jurchen people from Manchuria, further to the north. Some fifty years ago his ancestors conquered half of China. They called their dynasty (ruling family) the Jin, which means 'golden'.

guards patrol the city walls

Europeans will later copy this Chinese silk winding machine to create spinning wheels.

farmers prepare to leave their homes

these workers are using a chain pump to lift up lots of water quickly

wheelbarrows with sails carry larger loads

food shop

laundry

surveyors use a water level to set out the building site

horses and camels transport passengers and their luggage

a Jurchen official

small workshop

many people are forced out of their homes against their will

Chain pumps lift water from ditches, for use in building or for irrigating (watering) fields of crops.

Around 1150 the Jin moved their capital here, and named it Zhongdu ('central capital'). They repaired and rebuilt it, and now they are again expanding the city. Jin officials begin to clear the area that will be enclosed by the new walls. Soon labourers will start 'creating mountains' – shaping a hilly, landscaped park where once there was only flat farmland.

wooden scaffolding allows builders to work safely on the high walls

builders have no winches, but use levers to lift heavy loads

sighting board and poles help to keep walls in line

The Chinese people are made to shave the tops of their heads as their Jurchen leaders do.

huge wagons carry materials for building the city and its walls – some are pulled by up to 500 workers

a heavy brickwork facing protects the wall's core of rammed earth

this wall will be demolished as the city expands

provisions are brought into Zhongdu

Jurchen officials visit the farmhouse to evict the owners

the city walls are 32km in length

roof timbers support glazed tiles in a distinctive curved shape

the local people go about their daily business as best they can

Jin palace
1200CE

Just to the southwest of the spot where the old farming village once stood, there is now a tall, handsome pavilion. It is the home of a wealthy Zhongdu merchant. The outer walls enclose a vast area of buildings and open spaces. As well as houses for the city's rich and noble families, there are tradesmen's workshops and market streets.

Not far away, in the centre of the city, the Jin palace outshines even the grandest houses. It glitters with decorations of pure gold and brilliantly colourful paint. More than a million workers built the palace at huge expense. They used materials plundered from the old capital of Kaifeng, 600km away. Just moving one of the huge roof timbers cost one man's weight in silver.

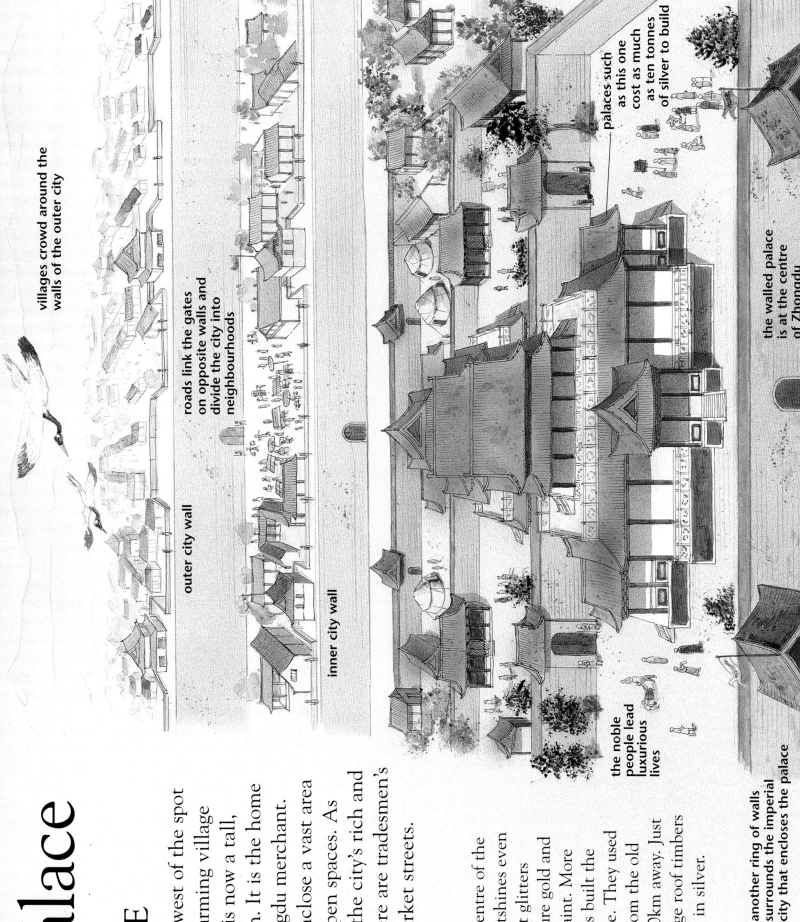

villages crowd around the walls of the outer city

roads link the gates on opposite walls and divide the city into neighbourhoods

outer city wall

inner city wall

palaces such as this one cost as much as ten tonnes of silver to build

the noble people lead luxurious lives

the walled palace is at the centre of Zhongdu

another ring of walls surrounds the imperial city that encloses the palace

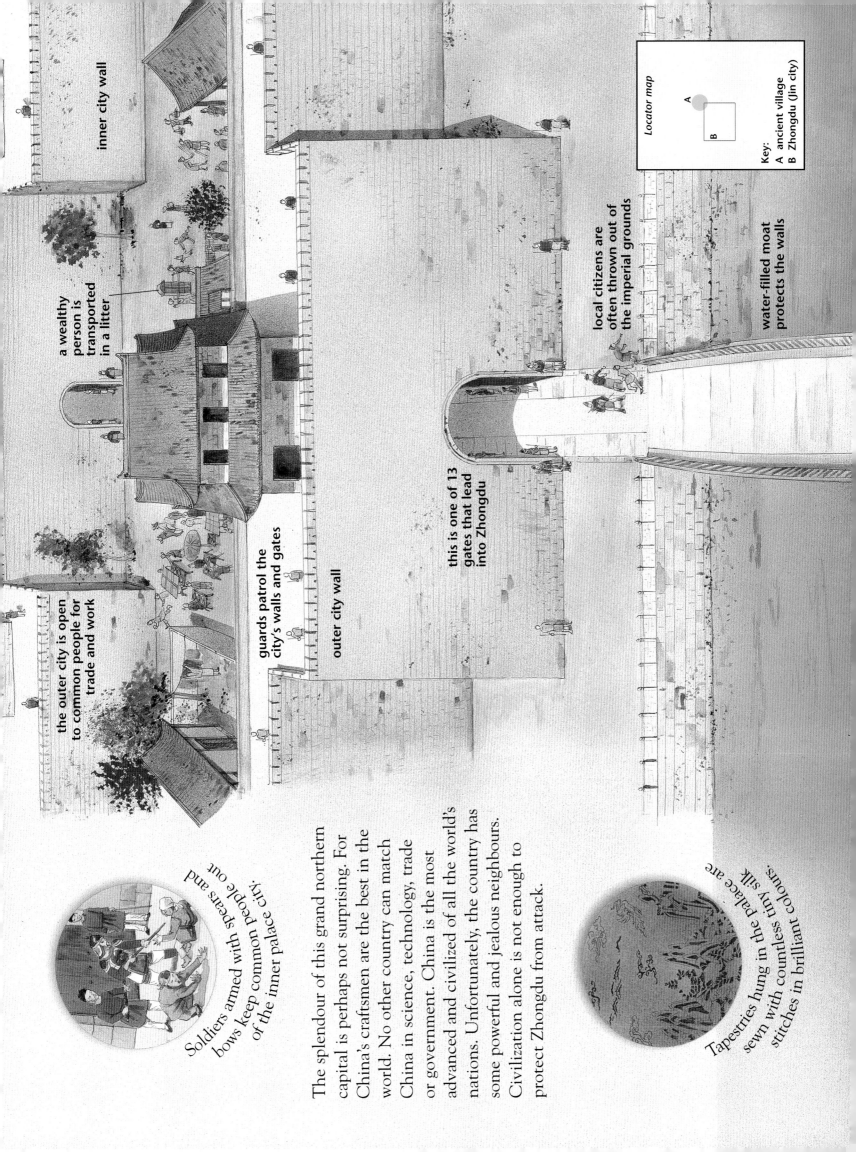

inner city wall

a wealthy person is transported in a litter

the outer city is open to common people for trade and work

guards patrol the city's walls and gates

outer city wall

this is one of 13 gates that lead into Zhongdu

local citizens are often thrown out of the imperial grounds

water-filled moat protects the walls

Locator map

A

B

Key:
A ancient village
B Zhongdu (Jin city)

Soldiers armed with spears and bows keep common people out of the inner palace city.

The splendour of this grand northern capital is perhaps not surprising. For China's craftsmen are the best in the world. No other country can match China in science, technology, trade or government. China is the most advanced and civilized of all the world's nations. Unfortunately, the country has some powerful and jealous neighbours. Civilization alone is not enough to protect Zhongdu from attack.

Tapestries hung in the palace are sewn with countless tiny silk stitches in brilliant colours.

Mongol tents surround the city

outer city wall

the skill, obedience and organization of the invaders help them capture the city

sick of their rulers, many Jin citizens and soldiers support and help the invaders

the warriors' diet includes the blood of their horses and cheese made from horse milk

the defending army is worn down by months and months of siege warfare

inner city wall

the city falls only after Genghis Khan personally takes command

it is late spring, but there is still snow on the ground in this chilly northern city

the Mongols light fires that burn for more than a month

rocks fired from trebuchets devastate the inner and imperial city walls

the city's defenders give way when they learn that their allies will not rescue them

Genghis Khan (c. 1165–1227) unites warring Mongol tribes and builds the world's biggest empire.

tents pitched in the palace grounds are a reminder that the Jin were once a wandering, nomadic people

Mongol conquest 1215 CE

the invading army uses huge trebuchets to hurl missiles over walls

Genghis ends his first siege of the city after the Jin emperor gives him gold, silk, horses... and his daughter!

Genghis Khan is the leader of the Mongol people, who rule the wild lands north of Zhongdu. 'One sun in the sky, one king on the earth!' is the Great Khan's motto. As his power grows, so do the fears of the Jin people. They know that, one day, he will plunder their glittering city.

That day comes in 1215, when the Mongol army besieges (surrounds and cuts off) Zhongdu. It is the second Mongol attack on the capital. The previous year, Genghis Khan spared the city in exchange for a bribe – and a bride. This time he is not so easily satisfied. Famine, flood, drought and war have weakened the Jin empire. On Wednesday 31 May, the city surrenders.

The invaders waste no time. First they strip the city of all its valuable items. Then they burn the beautiful palaces and pavilions. In just hours the fine houses built near the site of the ancient village are reduced to heaps of smoking ash. At first, those who survive the terrible attack rejoice. Soon, though, they envy the dead. Without food, they must eat human flesh to survive!

expert archers and horsemen, the Mongol warriors shoot from the saddle

Mongol soldiers slaughter the city's citizens and defenders trapped inside the walls

imperial city wall

fire spreads quickly through the dry wood frames of the grand palace buildings

flaming arrows set fire to the palace

Kublai Khan's city 1290CE

only Yuan officials and the wealthy are allowed to live within the city walls

After the capture and ruin of Zhongdu, the city is neglected for some 45 years. Then, in 1260, the Mongol people choose Genghis Khan's grandson, Kublai Khan (1215–94), to lead the Yuan dynasty. Six years later he begins to build a new capital city, close to the old city of Zhongdu. By 1290, it is a shining symbol of Mongol rule.

Called Dadu ('great capital'), the new city rises a little way to the northeast. The spot where the old village once stood is now just inside Dadu's walls. All around, glorious new palaces and pavilions rise up. Much bigger than Zhongdu, Dadu has a moat around its earth walls, and wide streets laid out in a grid pattern.

the emperor and his family live on an island in the Taiye Lake, which is all that remains of the Jin city

Taiye Lake (or North Lake)

Marco Polo (1254–1324) spends 17 years in China. For some years, he works as an official for the Khan.

To bring food to Dadu from distant farms, Khan commands three million workers to extend the Grand Canal.

a waterway links the city's lakes to the Grand Canal

As the capital, Dadu attracts attention from all over China – and beyond. Among the first European visitors is Marco Polo, a trader from the Italian city of Venice. He is impressed, saying that the palace is '…so vast, so rich and so beautiful, that no man on earth could design anything better'. When he returns to Europe, Marco's descriptions of China will make him famous.

Kublai Khan's sons live in grand Mongol tents outside the walls of the palace city

16

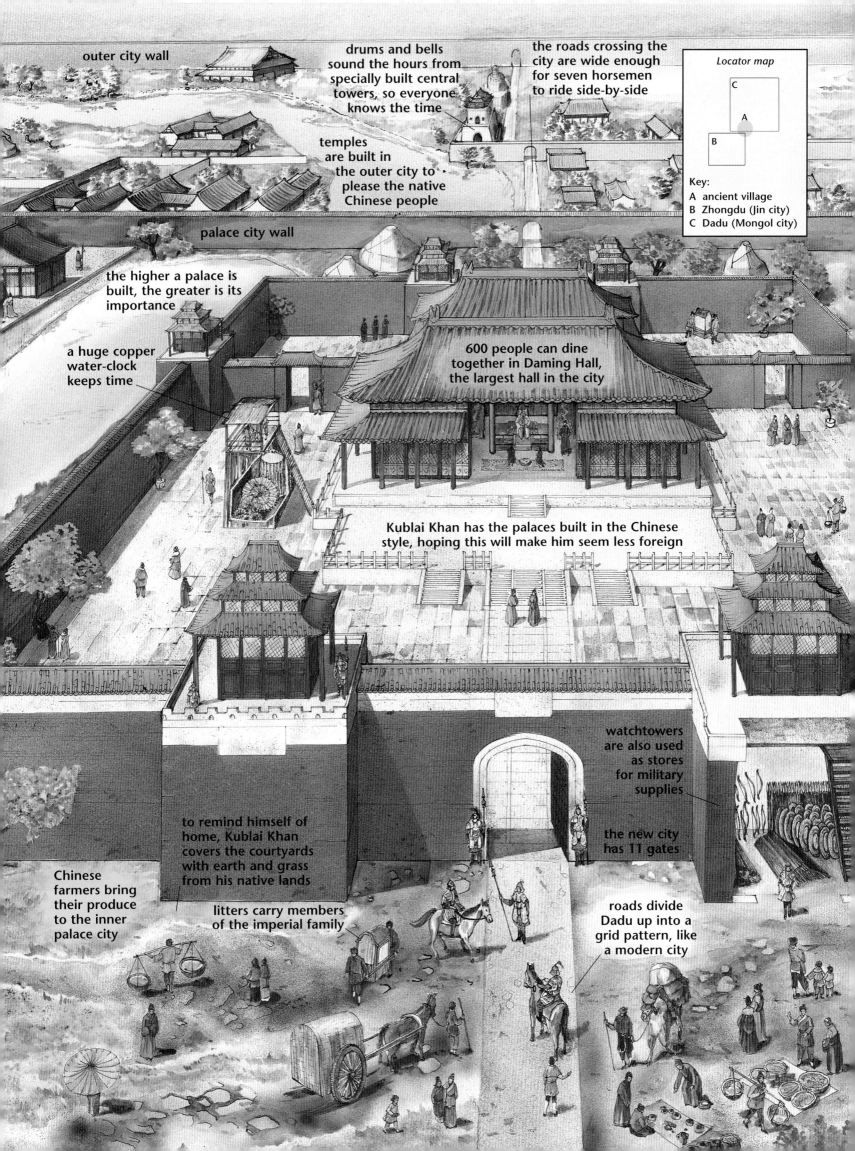

outer city wall

drums and bells sound the hours from specially built central towers, so everyone knows the time

the roads crossing the city are wide enough for seven horsemen to ride side-by-side

temples are built in the outer city to please the native Chinese people

Locator map

Key:
A ancient village
B Zhongdu (Jin city)
C Dadu (Mongol city)

palace city wall

the higher a palace is built, the greater is its importance

a huge copper water-clock keeps time

600 people can dine together in Daming Hall, the largest hall in the city

Kublai Khan has the palaces built in the Chinese style, hoping this will make him seem less foreign

watchtowers are also used as stores for military supplies

the new city has 11 gates

to remind himself of home, Kublai Khan covers the courtyards with earth and grass from his native lands

Chinese farmers bring their produce to the inner palace city

litters carry members of the imperial family

roads divide Dadu up into a grid pattern, like a modern city

Ming conquest 1368CE

Mongol rule of China is brief. The emperors who follow Kublai Khan are not as clever as he was. By the middle of the 14th century CE the Chinese people are fed up with their failing government. Millions of poor people are starving. Yet inside Dadu's pavilions there are corrupt and dishonest Yuan officials living in luxury.

The miserable conditions are not entirely the fault of the officials in charge. Floods, famine and deadly diseases have made life hard for the Chinese people. But the government has failed to help. To pay for emergency relief work, they raise taxes and print so much money that the banknotes become worthless. Also, they cannot stop the bandits who are attacking and robbing towns everywhere.

In a distant part of the city, Dadu's terrified and defeated rulers flee towards Mongolia.

Chinese people who want an end to foreign rule join together and gather weapons. A rebel army, called the Red Turbans, heads for Dadu. The rebels are well equipped, well trained and very determined. Dadu's defenders are weak and weary. In September 1368 they surrender. Unlike the city's Mongol conquerors, the rebels try not to cause too much damage. They even preserve the palaces at the city's centre.

palace city wall

Yuan troops struggle to defend just the innermost walled palace city from attack

hungry, and tired of high taxes, the local people welcome the rebel army

Yuan troops had been sent away to crush distant rebellions, so there are too few left to defend the capital

rammed-earth walls soon decay unless they are constantly repaired

the defending Yuan soldiers use their own catapults to return missiles hurled at the city by the rebels

outer city wall

Chinese citizens flee to safety

the rebels' artillery includes large cannons such as this one

some fires rage, but most of the city is undamaged in the attack

both the defending and attacking soldiers use recently invented firearms

The rebel leader, Zhu Yuanzhang, (1328–98), began life as a cowhand, but becomes the first Ming emperor.

inner city wall

a disease may have weakened the defending Yuan army before the attack began

the gates have double walls, but even these defences cannot stop the invading rebels

the rebel soldiers wear red turbans

the rebels are tough soldiers who have been fighting the Yuan for years

the city's water supply has been neglected, so the moat provides little protection

siege tower

The Forbidden City
1406CE

Once the rebels' victory over the hated Yuan is complete, they become China's new rulers, the Ming. They also begin a new dynasty, the Ming. Though at first they abandon Dadu, the city becomes China's chief city again in 1403. It gets a new name, too: Beijing, meaning 'northern capital'.

Three years later work begins here on a new palace. Craftsmen start by tearing down the existing buildings. In their place rises a fabulous 'city within a city'. Inside its walls the third Ming emperor will rule like a god. Only those he chooses may enter or leave. Locked and guarded gates will keep out the ordinary citizens, so this rich palace city is named the Forbidden City.

barges and ships break the ice of the frozen waterways to bring materials

new laws made grain-carrying ships, sailing to the city, also take on loads of bricks

massive logs brought from forests up to 1,500km away

brick works spew out foul smoke, so they are positioned down-wind, to the southwest of the city

Workers create roads of ice, so that they can slide massive stone blocks, weighing 180 tonnes, to the palace.

roofs are covered in brilliantly shiny glazed yellow tiles

all the building work is supervised by Nguyen An, a eunuch. (see page 22)

decorators pick out the finest details in real gold

the Palace of Heavenly Purity rises next to the spot where the ancient village once stood

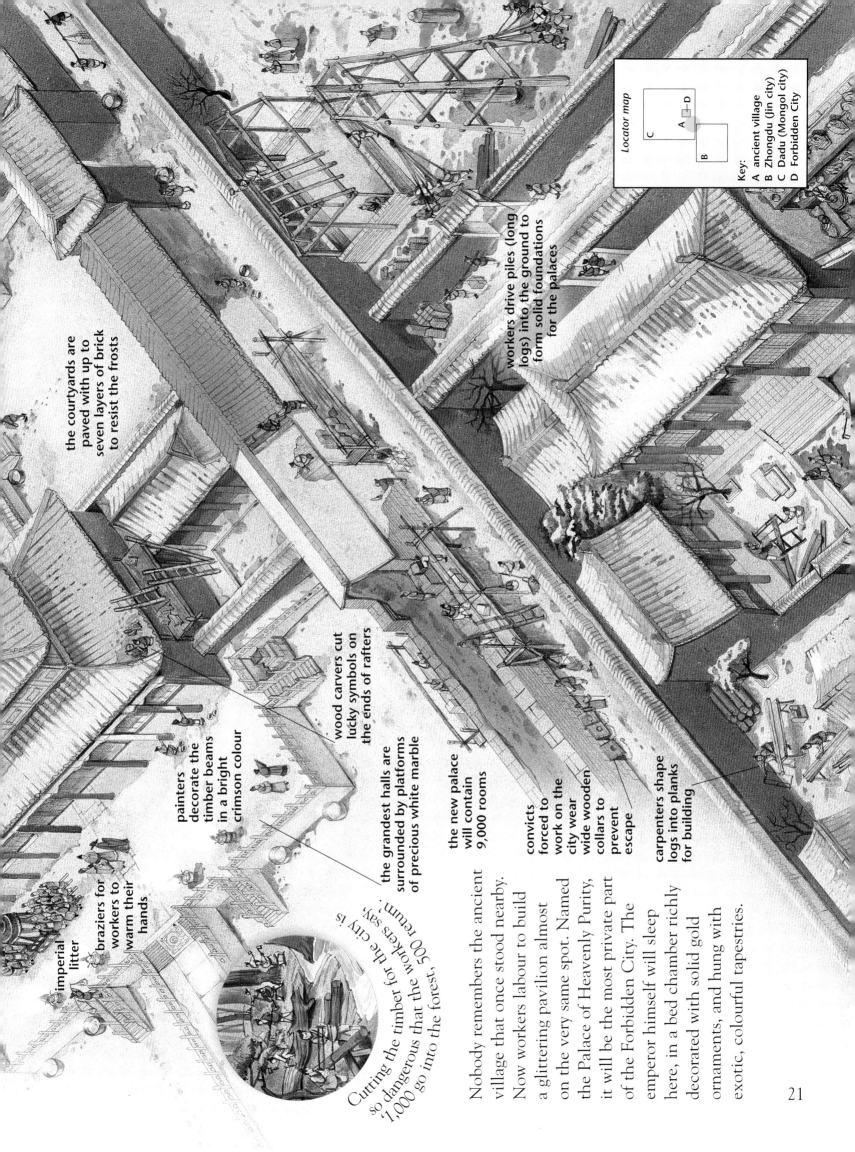

Locator map

Key:
A ancient village
B Zhongdu (Jin city)
C Dadu (Mongol city)
D Forbidden City

the courtyards are paved with up to seven layers of brick to resist the frosts

workers drive piles (long logs) into the ground to form solid foundations for the palaces

wood carvers cut lucky symbols on the ends of rafters

painters decorate the timber beams in a bright crimson colour

imperial litter

braziers for workers to warm their hands

the grandest halls are surrounded by platforms of precious white marble

the new palace will contain 9,000 rooms

convicts forced to work on the city wear wide wooden collars to prevent escape

carpenters shape logs into planks for building

Cutting the timber for the city is so dangerous that they say, '1,000 go into the forest, 500 workers return.'

Nobody remembers the ancient village that once stood nearby. Now workers labour to build a glittering pavilion almost on the very same spot. Named the Palace of Heavenly Purity, it will be the most private part of the Forbidden City. The emperor himself will sleep here, in a bed chamber richly decorated with solid gold ornaments, and hung with exotic, colourful tapestries.

21

Life in the palace 1480CE

Seated on a magnificent throne, the Ming Emperor Chenghua celebrates his birthday. The empress is one of his guests, as is her rival, Lady Wan. Once the emperor's nurse, and then his lover, Lady Wan is the scheming genius who truly controls the Forbidden City. The hall is crowded – but most of the guests are eunuchs, the civil servants who run the business of government.

Ming officials collect high taxes, even from the poorest country people.

the Hall of Complete Harmony is where the emperor puts on his imperial robes for special state occasions

the emperor's private apartments are situated behind his grand throne rooms

the Hall of Supreme Harmony is the biggest pavilion in the Forbidden City

the emperor's throne is covered in gold

Emperor Chenghua

the empress

Lady Wan

the emperor's most trusted eunuchs have been his friends since childhood

the ramps are carved with images of mythical creatures

only one of the emperor's children will escape Lady Wan's assassins

the Hall of Preserving Harmony is where the emperor greets foreign rulers, and also contains a lavish throne area

The emperor crushes any opposition to his rule with execution and imprisonment.

Most of the emperor's finely dressed courtiers were born male, but they never grew to be men. To get jobs in the palace, they had to undergo an operation called castration. People who have had this operation are known as eunuchs, and they are unable to have children. The eunuchs are powerful, but their power dies with them. They will never have sons to threaten the emperor's authority.

servants carry the emperor into the halls on a sedan chair, up a marble ramp

eunuchs bustle everywhere, attending to various duties

10,000 eunuchs now work in the Forbidden City, and their numbers will grow to 70,000

very junior eunuchs do chores such as cleaning

Lady Wan jealously guards her power – even bribing assassins to poison the emperor's children.

the eunuchs control the workshops and storehouses among the Forbidden City's 800 buildings

court attendants parade decorative lanterns

apart from the imperial family, only women and eunuchs are allowed to live in the Forbidden City

Chenghua was only 16 when he became emperor, and he has never learned to rule wisely. Following Lady Wan's advice, he promotes greedy and corrupt eunuchs to high positions. He takes his people's lands to pay for his life of luxury in the palace. But though he is a weak ruler, and too fond of the good life, Chenghua is certainly not the worst of the Ming emperors.

Fire!
1514CE

It begins with an almighty bang. Tents full of gunpowder, standing ready for a make-believe battle, have caught fire. Soon there are tongues of flame licking around the largest pavilions of the Forbidden City. As the heat melts the frost of the crisp February night, Emperor Zhengde laughs: 'That's one big fire!' he says, and then goes off to bed.

The emperor loves to play war and hunting games in the city... until he is badly injured by a tiger.

Zhengde does not care about the fire. The tenth of the mighty Ming emperors, he lives only for pleasure. He is not at all interested in governing China and its people. Instead he wastes his days in the company of beautiful women. The fire begins because a military commander, called the Prince of Ning, is trying to impress the emperor. Knowing of his love for lanterns, the prince has sent him hundreds. A spark from one of them sets the gunpowder alight.

the imperial gardens

the fire takes hold quickly because most of the buildings are made entirely of wood

the Palace of Earthly Tranquillity

the flames of the burning palace can be seen from many kilometres away

the emperor lives outside the Forbidden City, in a new private palace to the northwest

the explosions set fire to surrounding buildings

tents storing weapons and barrels of gunpowder

the Prince of Ning's servants light the lanterns

24

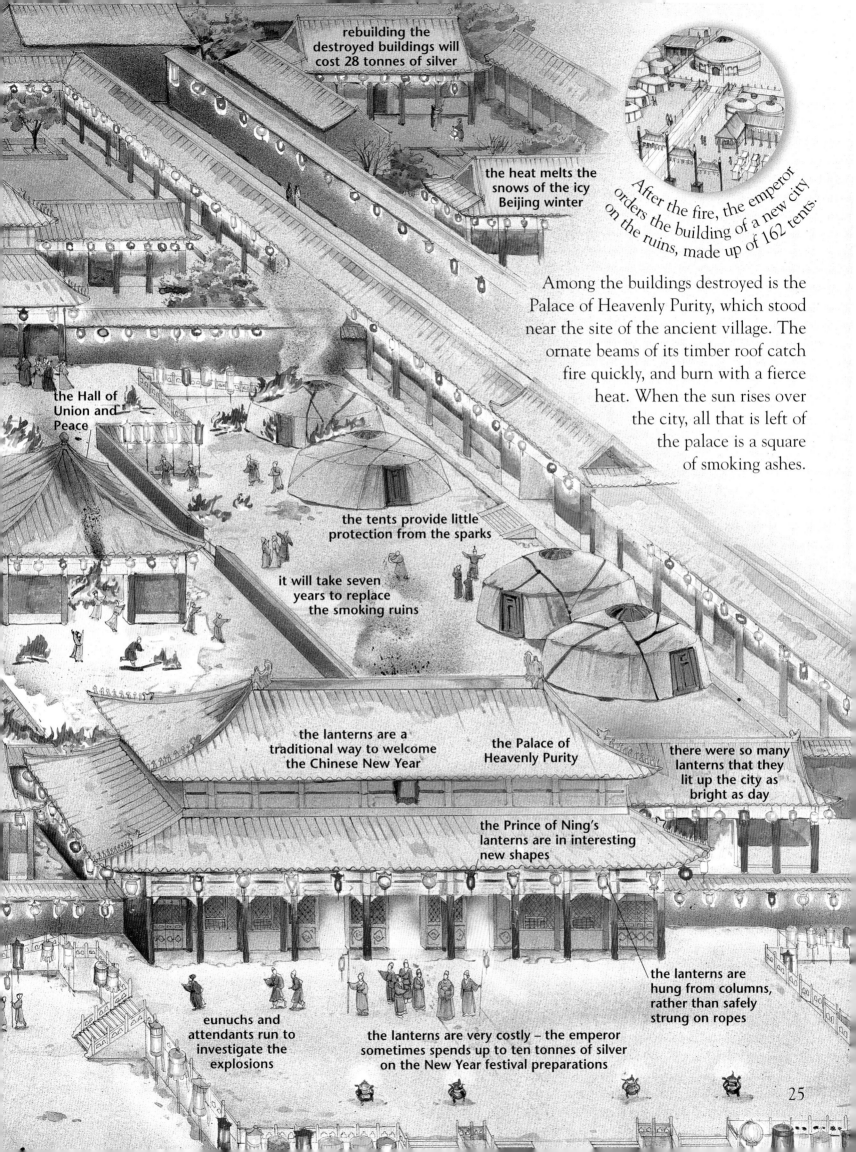

rebuilding the destroyed buildings will cost 28 tonnes of silver

the heat melts the snows of the icy Beijing winter

After the fire, the emperor orders the building of a new city on the ruins, made up of 162 tents.

Among the buildings destroyed is the Palace of Heavenly Purity, which stood near the site of the ancient village. The ornate beams of its timber roof catch fire quickly, and burn with a fierce heat. When the sun rises over the city, all that is left of the palace is a square of smoking ashes.

the Hall of Union and Peace

the tents provide little protection from the sparks

it will take seven years to replace the smoking ruins

the lanterns are a traditional way to welcome the Chinese New Year

the Palace of Heavenly Purity

there were so many lanterns that they lit up the city as bright as day

the Prince of Ning's lanterns are in interesting new shapes

the lanterns are hung from columns, rather than safely strung on ropes

eunuchs and attendants run to investigate the explosions

the lanterns are very costly – the emperor sometimes spends up to ten tonnes of silver on the New Year festival preparations

25

The leader of the rebel army, Li Zicheng, trained as a despatch rider in the emperor's postal service.

any rebel soldiers caught looting or harming citizens are executed on the spot by their superiors

the rebel soldiers take over the palaces near to where the ancient village once stood

the Palace of Earthly Tranquillity

Locator map

C
A — D
B
E

Key:
A ancient village
B Zhongdu (Jin city)
C Dadu (Mongol city)
D Forbidden City
E Beijing (Ming city)

the emperor fled through this gate in the north wall of the Forbidden City – he had originally planned to flee the city disguised as a eunuch

the rebel army takes over the Forbidden City calmly and with little damage

the emperor's loyal eunuch prepares a chain, which the emperor will use to take his own life

In his final speech, Emperor Chongzhen says, 'I gave my people decency, why do none support me?'

the emperor hangs himself from a branch of a pagoda tree known as the Guilty Chinese Scholar tree

the emperor discards his ceremonial clothes before ending his life

Fall of the Ming 1644 CE

Ming soldiers are away protecting the border, leaving Beijing's walls completely undefended

the rebel troops have overrun Beijing – they occupy the outer city first

the emperor ends his life on Coal Hill, a low mound to the north of the city

a pavilion nearby on Coal Hill houses the imperial 'hat and girdle department'

labourers created Coal Hill from the soil they dug out to form the Forbidden City's lakes and moat

Chongzhen is proud of the Ming dynasty that has made him its 16th emperor. Under the Ming, China has grown strong, wealthy and peaceful. Their sailors have explored the ocean in huge ships. Trade, technology and science have thrived under Ming control. The Great Wall, which the Ming built to keep out foreigners, will still be standing in 350 years time.

Most of these great advances took place long ago. Chongzhen himself is weak and unpopular. Danger threatens from inside and outside of the country. In 1644 a rebel army surrounds Beijing, and on China's borders another army gathers. The Manchus, a Jurchen people, are ready to invade and seize power. Chongzhen knows he will soon be defeated.

When Chongzhen's daughter refuses to end her life, the furious emperor orders her arm cut off.

The shame of failure is too much for Chongzhen. He calls his family together in the Forbidden City and orders them to kill themselves. The empress and others obey him, hanging themselves from rafters in the fine pavilions. Then, at around midnight on 25 April, Chongzhen climbs a hill behind the city. Helped by a loyal eunuch, he hangs himself from a tree.

the Russian visitors are very impressed by the emperor's elephants

the Qing rebuild many of the Forbidden City's palaces and pavilions – as exact copies of the Ming originals

Jesuit priests, also originally from Europe, attend the banquet with the Russian visitors

200 Qing officials surround the palace while the Russians dine with the emperor

European visitors 1695CE

The Forbidden City is a Chinese capital without Chinese people. Soon after occupying Beijing, and beginning the Qing dynasty, the Manchu invaders throw all Chinese people out of the inner city. To remind their subjects who is in charge, the emperor – called Kangxi – orders everyone to wear their hair in pigtails, which is the Manchu style.

Travelling from Europe to the Forbidden City has taken the Russians more than a year.

by giving this palace its original Ming name, the 'Hall of Supreme Harmony', the Qing show their respect for Chinese traditions

later, inside the palace, the Russians toast the emperor with drinks made from fermented horse milk

Jesuit (Catholic) priests from Europe, now living in Beijing, act as translators for the Russian visitors.

the Forbidden City buildings, restored by the Qing, will survive unchanged for more than 350 years

the Hall of Supreme Harmony

the Gate of Supreme Harmony

the Russians admire the huge size and lavish decoration of the palace

the Russians show their respect by leaving their horses outside the city walls

the Russian group leader, Evert Ides, brings greetings from the Russian tsar (ruler), Peter the Great

the foreign officials are enthralled by their visit, but the emperor is less impressed – after meeting them, he describes the Russians as 'narrow-minded and obstinate'

flags identify the 'bannermen' – official representatives of the eight Manchu clans that control China

As if this was not insulting enough, the Qing officials have begun to welcome the foreigners that Chinese people traditionally dislike. European Christian missionaries come to Beijing. The emperor himself learns about the Bible. He allows Christian priests to build churches in the city. In 1695 – after 40 years of trying – Russian officials finally get to meet the emperor.

At the dinner with the emperor, dishes of pork, mutton and goose are served to his foreign guests.

Emperor Kangxi greets his Russian visitors in one of the Forbidden City's grandest palaces. He throws a lavish banquet, and entertains them with jugglers, acrobats and musicians. Following the Russian visit, officials from other European nations will come to Beijing. By welcoming them all, the emperor makes a dangerous mistake that will change his country forever.

Western troops invade 1860CE

Once China began to welcome foreign traders, Chinese tea soon filled the stores of Europe. However, the Chinese bought very little from the Europeans. Hungry for profits, British merchants begin smuggling a drug called opium to China. Millions of Chinese become addicted. After Emperor Xianfeng tries to ban the drug in 1820, the British government sends an army to force China to buy opium and other goods.

the Forbidden City's pavilions will burn like the Summer Palaces if the Chinese do not give the Europeans what they want

the British officers set up their headquarters in a Buddhist temple south of the Forbidden City

the Forbidden City

Coal Hill

the emperor's half-brother, Prince Gong, stays in the city to make a deal with the French and English

the outskirts of Beijing

French and British troops also loot Beijing, outside the Forbidden City

at their camp, French soldiers decorate their tents with brilliantly coloured silks and embroidery, stolen from the palaces

British cavalry soldiers start fires in the Summer Palace grounds on 18 October, 1860 – around 40 palaces will be burned to the ground

just before the fires begin, one soldier describes the palaces as 'a fairyland'

Locator map
F○

Key:
A ancient village
B Zhongdu (Jin city)
C Dadu (Mongol city)
D Forbidden City
E Beijing (Qing city)
F Summer Palaces

the Summer Palaces

The second war starts in 1856 after Chinese officials board a smuggling ship and tear a British flag.

In the 'Opium War' that follows, Chinese troops face European warships, rifles and cannons. They are easily defeated, but a second war begins in 1856. This time British and French troops fight all the way to Beijing. The Chinese soldiers have been weakened by fighting a rebellion of their own people. They soon surrender and the emperor flees.

The foreign armies are furious that the Chinese have tortured and killed 25 English and French officials. To get their revenge, they allow their soldiers to loot the emperor's Summer Palaces, northwest of Beijing. Then they set the wooden pavilions aflame. The fires burn for several days. When the ashes cool, nothing is left of the beautiful buildings and the magnificent antiques that the looters had left behind.

flames will burn many of the countless valuables that the looters leave behind

the beautiful palace gardens survive to become a popular tourist attraction in future years

back at their camp, the British officers auction (sell to bidders) what they steal from the Summer Palaces

the governor of the palaces is so ashamed of the plunder that he later drowns himself in a pond

The emperor flees with his closest advisors, and will die within one year of the attack on Beijing.

looters throw what they cannot carry into the lakes, so that they can collect them later

soldiers strip the metal from the roofs and discover that it is pure gold

the looters smash any giant and ancient vases they cannot carry

The Boxer Rebellion 1900CE

As the 20th century begins, the Forbidden City is no longer the home of China's emperor, Tongzhi. He lives on an island nearby, imprisoned there by Cixi, his aunt. It is Cixi, not the emperor, who truly rules the country. Cunning and ruthless, she has clung to power for 40 years, but she is now facing a major crisis in Beijing.

The Chinese people want to kick out the foreigners they feel are ruining their country. A kung-fu society called the 'Boxers' has led a rebellion. Foolishly, Cixi supports them. A murderous army of Boxers floods into Beijing. Foreigners and Chinese Christians flee from them. They hide just outside the Forbidden City, in the legations (offices) of the foreign governments.

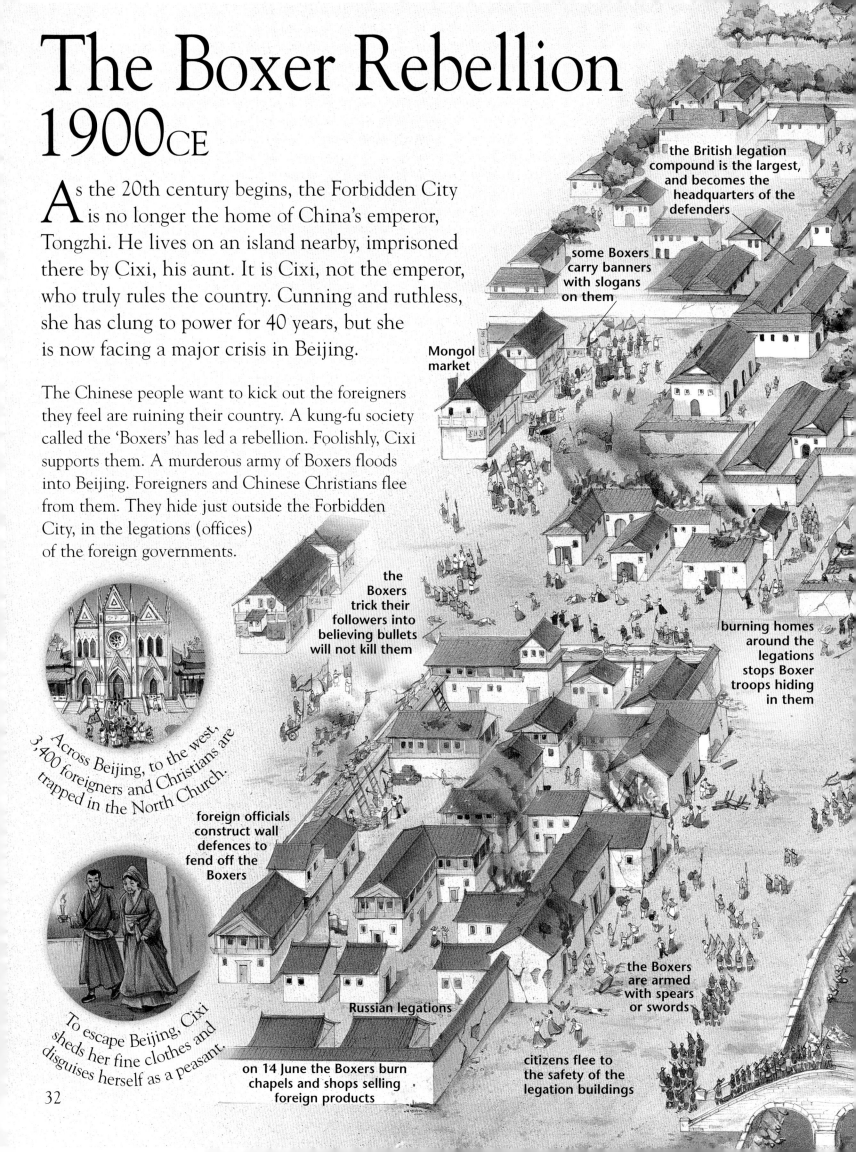

the British legation compound is the largest, and becomes the headquarters of the defenders

some Boxers carry banners with slogans on them

Mongol market

the Boxers trick their followers into believing bullets will not kill them

burning homes around the legations stops Boxer troops hiding in them

Across Beijing, to the west, 3,400 foreigners and Christians are trapped in the North Church.

foreign officials construct wall defences to fend off the Boxers

the Boxers are armed with spears or swords

To escape Beijing, Cixi sheds her fine clothes and disguises herself as a peasant.

Russian legations

on 14 June the Boxers burn chapels and shops selling foreign products

citizens flee to the safety of the legation buildings

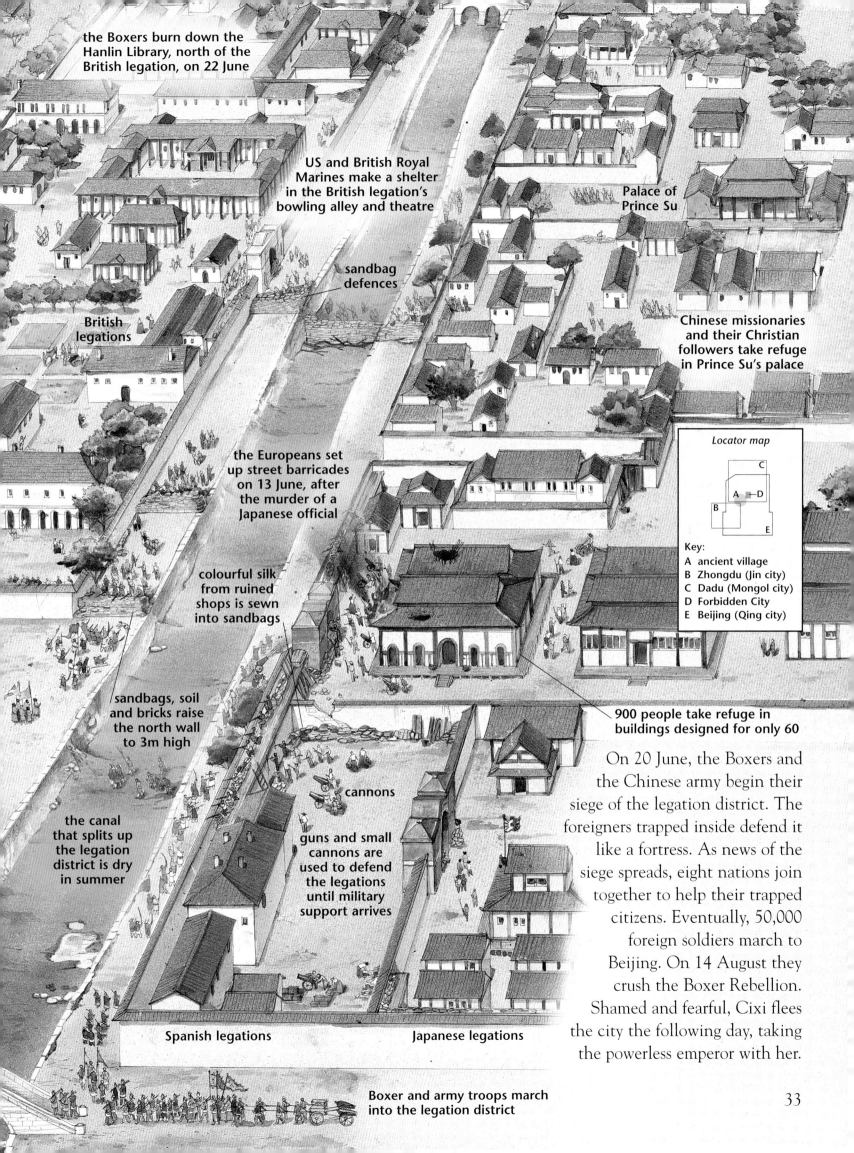

the Boxers burn down the Hanlin Library, north of the British legation, on 22 June

US and British Royal Marines make a shelter in the British legation's bowling alley and theatre

sandbag defences

Palace of Prince Su

British legations

Chinese missionaries and their Christian followers take refuge in Prince Su's palace

the Europeans set up street barricades on 13 June, after the murder of a Japanese official

Locator map

Key:
A ancient village
B Zhongdu (Jin city)
C Dadu (Mongol city)
D Forbidden City
E Beijing (Qing city)

colourful silk from ruined shops is sewn into sandbags

sandbags, soil and bricks raise the north wall to 3m high

900 people take refuge in buildings designed for only 60

cannons

the canal that splits up the legation district is dry in summer

guns and small cannons are used to defend the legations until military support arrives

On 20 June, the Boxers and the Chinese army begin their siege of the legation district. The foreigners trapped inside defend it like a fortress. As news of the siege spreads, eight nations join together to help their trapped citizens. Eventually, 50,000 foreign soldiers march to Beijing. On 14 August they crush the Boxer Rebellion. Shamed and fearful, Cixi flees the city the following day, taking the powerless emperor with her.

Spanish legations

Japanese legations

Boxer and army troops march into the legation district

33

though Puyi spends much of his lessons just chatting to his tutor, he finds time to learn how to read, write and speak English

Reginald Johnston is the first foreigner to enter the most sacred palaces of the Forbidden City.

Puyi sits facing south – in China this is thought to be the luckiest of all directions

for the first nine weeks of Puyi's studies, a Chinese tutor or official watches the lessons – and often falls asleep

Puyi cuts off his traditional plait when he hears Johnston refer to it as a 'pigtail'

Puyi, aged 13

a bored eunuch attends every class so that Johnston is never alone with Puyi

Chinese tutor

Reginald Johnston, Puyi's Scottish tutor, will eventually become his closest and most trusted friend

Puyi's imperial cap

Johnston's hat and gloves

hat stands

Johnston notices that Puyi has very poor eyesight – so, in 1921, he becomes the first emperor ever to wear spectacles

Puyi reads Western books and newspapers, and is very keen to follow world events

The last emperor 1919 CE

Puyi's lessons take place in the imperial schoolroom, not far from where the ancient village once stood

For over 2,000 years, emperors have ruled China like gods. Then, in 1911, everything changes. The Chinese people decide that they will rule the country themselves, and seize power in a revolution. Foreign and unpopular, the Qing dynasty collapses. Suddenly, it is obvious that the emperor is not a god, but a human, just like any other Chinese child.

The emperor, Puyi, first sat on the Forbidden City's golden throne in 1908, at the age of two. He was chosen to rule by the Empress Cixi when his uncle, the previous emperor, died. After the revolution, the country's leaders agree that Puyi can carry on living in the Forbidden City. Eunuchs will continue to pamper him, as before. Everyone will still call him 'emperor', but Puyi will have none of the imperial powers of old.

the eunuchs in attendance should never stand with their backs turned to the young emperor

eunuchs tidy and clean the corridors while the emperor is busy with his lessons

Johnston believes that the constant attention and flattery of the eunuchs will harm the young emperor, and wants them removed from the lessons

Puyi prefers a modern bicycle to the traditional litters that carried former emperors around the city.

Puyi grows up in a strange world. Grovelling eunuchs follow him everywhere. He is not allowed to leave the Forbidden City. Gradually, though, he learns a little about the world outside its high walls. From 1919, a Scottish tutor called Reginald Johnston is employed to help him. As well as teaching him English, Johnston prepares Puyi for the day when his life as emperor will end. For without an empire, Puyi is not really an emperor at all.

When aged 17, Puyi bribes eunuchs to let him escape his city prison... but his plot fails.

35

A new age
1924CE

Locked away inside the Forbidden City, the boy-emperor Puyi becomes a man, and chooses a wife. As he grows older, and wiser, he sees that the eunuchs are stealing treasures from the palace stores, and lighting fires there to hide their crimes. Puyi expels them all from his court. He modernizes the Forbidden City, learning to use cars and telephones.

the army lays on a procession of cars to take the former emperor away

the last car brings Shao Ying, the controller of the imperial household

the rebels do not use the central gateway, as this is the imperial entrance – they wish to make it clear that Puyi no longer has imperial status

the third car carries Wan Jung, Puyi's wife and China's empress until moments before

soldiers have replaced the imperial guard at the gates of the Forbidden City

the rebel soldiers celebrate the removal of the last emperor of China

Puyi is driven in the second car

soldiers with pistols cling on to the outside of each car, with their feet on the running boards

Though Puyi expels the eunuchs, their thefts from the palace stores have already made them very rich.

an armed soldier sits next to each of the drivers

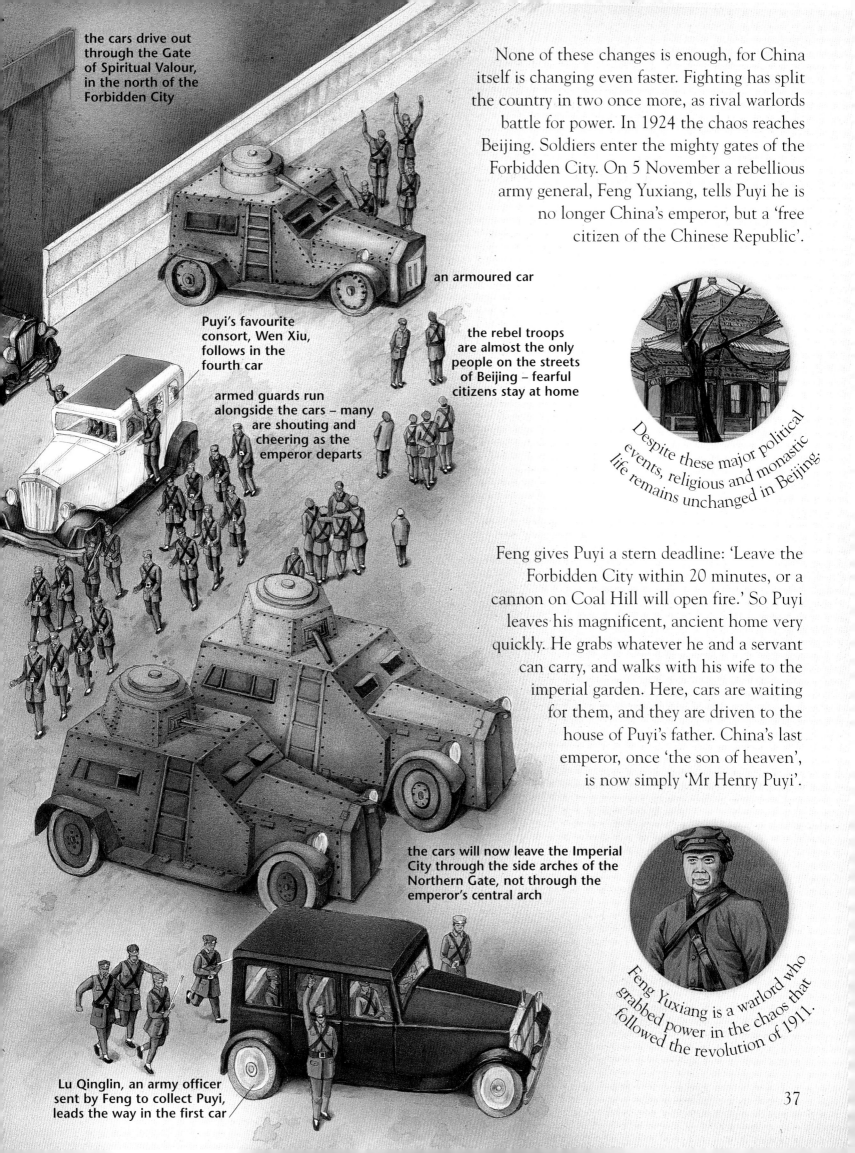

the cars drive out through the Gate of Spiritual Valour, in the north of the Forbidden City

None of these changes is enough, for China itself is changing even faster. Fighting has split the country in two once more, as rival warlords battle for power. In 1924 the chaos reaches Beijing. Soldiers enter the mighty gates of the Forbidden City. On 5 November a rebellious army general, Feng Yuxiang, tells Puyi he is no longer China's emperor, but a 'free citizen of the Chinese Republic'.

an armoured car

Puyi's favourite consort, Wen Xiu, follows in the fourth car

the rebel troops are almost the only people on the streets of Beijing – fearful citizens stay at home

armed guards run alongside the cars – many are shouting and cheering as the emperor departs

Despite these major political events, religious and monastic life remains unchanged in Beijing.

Feng gives Puyi a stern deadline: 'Leave the Forbidden City within 20 minutes, or a cannon on Coal Hill will open fire.' So Puyi leaves his magnificent, ancient home very quickly. He grabs whatever he and a servant can carry, and walks with his wife to the imperial garden. Here, cars are waiting for them, and they are driven to the house of Puyi's father. China's last emperor, once 'the son of heaven', is now simply 'Mr Henry Puyi'.

the cars will now leave the Imperial City through the side arches of the Northern Gate, not through the emperor's central arch

Feng Yuxiang is a warlord who grabbed power in the chaos that followed the revolution of 1911.

Lu Qinglin, an army officer sent by Feng to collect Puyi, leads the way in the first car

The Cultural Revolution 1966CE

Beijing's palace complex is forbidden no longer: it is open as a museum. Since the country's communist revolution began, the Forbidden City has stood for everything that was wrong with the 'old' China. In the new People's Republic, everyone is equal. There is no place for palaces, nor for emperors who rule like gods.

On 18 August 1966, the revolution takes a new and frightening turn. The Chairman of the Communist Party, Mao Zedong, has urged students to protest. He wants their support against his enemies, who he says are holding the country back. The students hold a vast rally just outside the Forbidden City. Calling themselves 'Red Guards', they violently attack anyone who opposes Mao.

Mao Zedong shows he approves of the Red Guards' violence when he agrees to wear their armband.

the rally is held in Tiananmen Square, right outside Tiananmen gate

staff and students have come to the rally from colleges all over China

During the Cultural Revolution, former emperor Puyi works in Beijing's public gardens.

portrait of Mao

many students carry posters with slogans attacking those who control the university

This large-scale rebellion is known as the Cultural Revolution. The Red Guards are trying to rid China of what they call the 'Four Olds': Old Customs, Old Culture, Old Habits and Old Ideas. Anyone who does not support Mao becomes a target. Intellectuals – people who do not work with their hands – are tortured and robbed. In just ten years, half a million people die. The Red Guards also attack historic sites, temples and precious antiques, but the Forbidden City escapes destruction.

On 19 August, Red Guards put up posters calling for the destruction of the Forbidden City.

Tiananmen (the Gate of Heavenly Peace) is the entrance to the Forbidden City

many of the vast crowd have been waiting since 1am, when the rally started

Mao and other Communist Party leaders arrive just after sunrise

there are almost a million people packed into the square

tens of thousands of Red Guards watch from stands on either side of Tiananmen

the parading columns march from the square at 11am

a sea of waving red flags greets Mao

the crowds roar 'Long live Chairman Mao!'

Museum city
Today

At the very heart of a bustling, busy, 21st-century Beijing, the Forbidden City stands out like an ancient and beautiful jewel. Renamed the Palace Museum, it attracts ten million visitors each year. Thanks to strict planning laws, no tall office blocks are allowed to be built where they might spoil the view of the splendid wooden pavilions.

during the Cultural Revolution, fewer than 80 of Beijing's 8,000 other historic buildings were protected from destruction

six in every ten of the golden glazed tiles needed replacing

restoration is a challenge because the hall is among the largest wooden buildings in the world

two sides of the roof were sinking

the Hall of Supreme Harmony was restored in 2006, for the first time since it was rebuilt by the Qing dynasty in 1697

the plans for the restoration are based on newly discovered 1,000-year-old documents

more than 1,300 museum staff look after the Forbidden City, instead of the eunuchs of old

24 emperors have climbed these steps to sit on the throne

Nicknamed the 'bird's nest', Beijing's Olympic stadium lies 8km north of the Forbidden City.

five out of every six visitors are Chinese

tour guides take visitors around the palace buildings

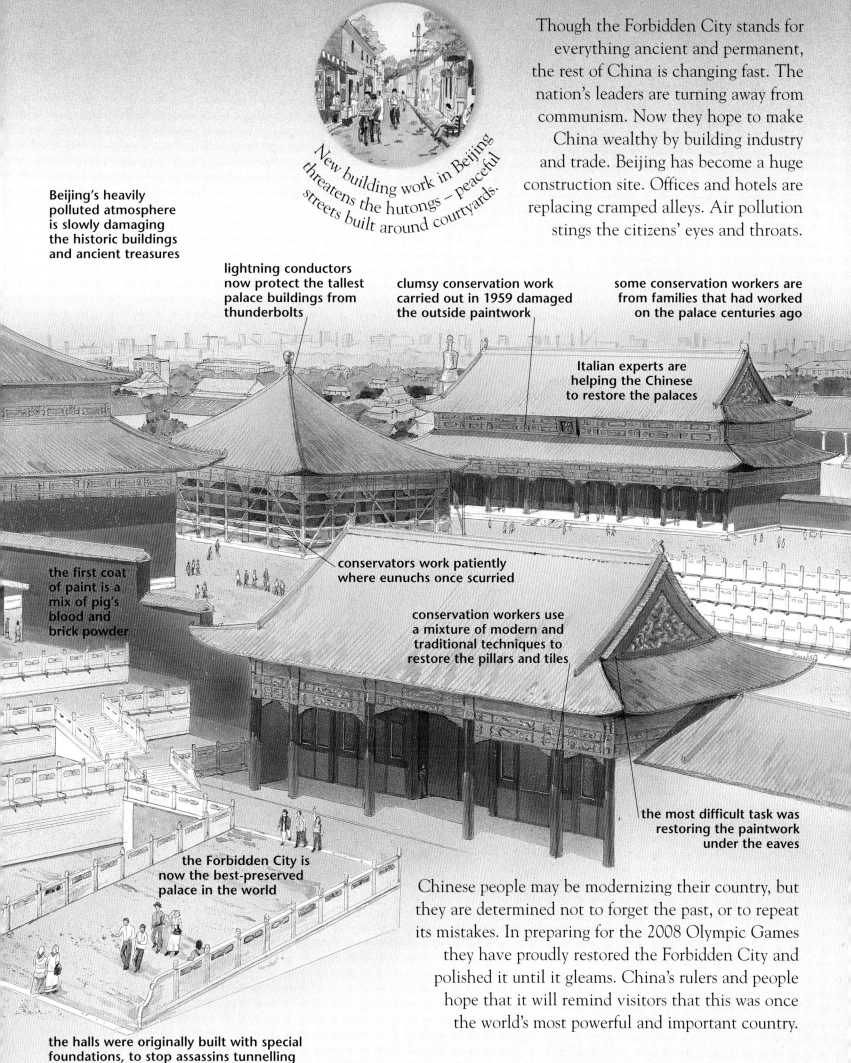

New building work in Beijing threatens the hutongs – peaceful streets built around courtyards.

Though the Forbidden City stands for everything ancient and permanent, the rest of China is changing fast. The nation's leaders are turning away from communism. Now they hope to make China wealthy by building industry and trade. Beijing has become a huge construction site. Offices and hotels are replacing cramped alleys. Air pollution stings the citizens' eyes and throats.

Beijing's heavily polluted atmosphere is slowly damaging the historic buildings and ancient treasures

lightning conductors now protect the tallest palace buildings from thunderbolts

clumsy conservation work carried out in 1959 damaged the outside paintwork

some conservation workers are from families that had worked on the palace centuries ago

Italian experts are helping the Chinese to restore the palaces

conservators work patiently where eunuchs once scurried

the first coat of paint is a mix of pig's blood and brick powder

conservation workers use a mixture of modern and traditional techniques to restore the pillars and tiles

the most difficult task was restoring the paintwork under the eaves

the Forbidden City is now the best-preserved palace in the world

Chinese people may be modernizing their country, but they are determined not to forget the past, or to repeat its mistakes. In preparing for the 2008 Olympic Games they have proudly restored the Forbidden City and polished it until it gleams. China's rulers and people hope that it will remind visitors that this was once the world's most powerful and important country.

the halls were originally built with special foundations, to stop assassins tunnelling in and harming the emperors

41

Glossary

A tent burns after an explosion in the Forbidden City in 1514.

Words in *italics* refer to other glossary entries.

ancestor
Someone's parents, and also their grandparents and great-grandparents, and so on, through to the oldest members of a family.

assassin
A murderer, especially one paid to kill an important person secretly or by surprise.

Beijing
The Chinese name for their capital city, first used by the *Ming dynasty*. It means 'northern capital'.

brazier
A small fire used for heating or cooking.

Buddhist
Someone who respects and follows the teachings of Buddha, the 6th-century BCE deep thinker.

castration
An operation that prevents men having children.

cavalry
A group of soldiers fighting on horseback.

Chenghua (1447–87)
The ninth *emperor* of the *Ming dynasty*.

Chinese New Year
A festival celebrated with lanterns at the start of each year, which begins in the spring in China.

Chinese Republic
The name for China after a revolution ended *Qing* rule in 1912.

Chongzhen (1611–44)
The sixteenth and last *emperor* of the *Ming dynasty*.

civil servant
Someone who works for the government.

Prehistoric marsh-dwellers shaped blades and jewellery out of stones, bones and shells.

Cixi, Empress Dowager (1835–1908)
Mother of the ninth *Qing emperor*, *Tongzhi*, and aunt of the tenth. She ruled China for nearly 50 years by controlling both of them.

clan
A family group that shares the same *ancestor*.

communism
A way of organizing a country so that its people govern themselves, and share equally in the country's wealth.

conservation
Looking after ancient buildings and treasures.

conservator
Someone who is skilled in *conservation*.

Rebel soldiers move a siege tower into position during their attack on Dadu in 1368.

consort
The husband, wife or unmarried partner of a ruler or important person.

Cultural Revolution (1966–76)
A time of disorder and chaos in China when *Mao Zedong* fought his rivals for power.

Dadu
The name, meaning 'great capital', given to the *Mongol* capital of China in the 13th century.

drought
A time when not enough rain falls for everyone to drink or grow food.

dynasty
A ruling family.

emperor
A ruler who controls a large region, and who has complete power over its people.

eunuch
A man who has been *castrated*.

famine
A time when many people die because there is not enough to eat.

Feng Yuxiang (1882–1948)
A general of the *Chinese Republic* who threw the last *emperor*, *Puyi*, out of the *Forbidden City*.

Forbidden City
The walled city of great palaces at the centre of *Beijing*, built by the *Ming*, which only the country's *emperors* and their families and servants could enter.

Genghis Khan (c.1165–1227)
A *Mongol* leader who led the conquest of China and greatly extended its borders.

Grand Canal
A waterway dug by China's *Mongol* rulers to bring food and supplies to *Beijing*.

Great Wall
The name for several stone and earth walls built from the 5th to the 16th centuries to protect China's northern border.

Hall of Complete Harmony
The smallest *pavilion* in the *Forbidden City*'s Outer Court, where the *emperor* rested and dressed before attending ceremonies in the other pavilions.

Hall of Preserving Harmony
A small *pavilion* in the *Forbidden City*'s Outer Court, used for greeting foreign rulers.

Hall of Supreme Harmony
The largest *pavilion* in the *Forbidden City*, where *Ming* and *Qing emperors* married and were crowned.

Hall of Union and Peace
A *pavilion* in the *Forbidden City* used to store 25 precious stone seals that *emperors* used to 'sign' official documents.

Homo erectus
This species (group) of humans lived some two million years ago, and was the first to walk erect or upright.

The marshland people made their clothes out of animal skins.

hutong
A neighbourhood of narrow streets in *Beijing*, where the houses are traditionally built around a courtyard. Hutongs were originally the homes of nobles.

Ides, Evert (1657–c.1708)
A Russian official who travelled from Moscow to *Beijing*. Evert Ides was among the first Europeans to meet a Chinese *emperor*, in 1695.

imperial
Anything associated with an empire or *emperor*.

Jesuits
A society of Roman Catholic priests and monks who introduced their Christian religion to *Beijing* in the 17th century.

Ji
The name for the ancient city that grew up 2,400 years ago, close to where *Beijing* now stands.

Jin
The *dynasty* name for the *Jurchen* people of *Manchuria*, who ruled half of China from the 12th century.

Johnston, Reginald (1874–1938)
A Scottish tutor who taught and advised China's last *emperor*, *Puyi*, in the early 20th century.

Jurchen
A people from *Manchuria*, who conquered half the country and ruled as the *Jin dynasty* from the 12th century.

Kangxi (1654–1722)
The fourth *emperor* of the *Qing dynasty*, who ruled China for longer than any other emperor.

When the Mongols ruled China, native Chinese farmers brought their produce to the capital city, Dadu.

The looting of the Summer Palaces, in 1860

Kublai Khan (1215–94)
The *Mongol* grandson of *Genghis Khan*. Kublai Khan built the city of *Dadu*.

Lady Wan (born c. 1430)
As nurse, and later the lover, of *Ming emperor Chenghua*, she gained great power and controlled the emperor.

Li Zicheng (1606–45)
The leader of the peasant army that rebelled against their *Ming* rulers, starting the *Qing dynasty*.

litter
A chair carried by servants, in which *emperors* and Chinese nobles travelled. Also known as a 'sedan chair'.

Manchu
The people of *Manchuria*, who conquered China in the 17th century and ruled as the *Qing dynasty*.

Manchuria
A country northeast of ancient China, now divided between Russia, Mongolia and China.

Mao Zedong (1893–1976)
Chairman of the Chinese Communist Party and leader of China for the last 27 years of his life.

marble
A type of very hard, beautiful stone, used for building and sculpture, that can be polished until shiny.

millet
A food plant, grown for its nourishing grain, that needs little water to thrive.

Ming
The *dynasty* that ruled China from 1368 to 1644.

A guard from emperor Kangxi's court

Mongolia
A large central Asian country, just north of China.

Mongols
The people of *Mongolia*, who conquered China in 1215.

nomadic
Wandering with no fixed home.

opium
A dangerous drug made from poppies, illegally sold to the Chinese people by European countries in the 18th and 19th centuries.

Palace of Earthly Tranquillity
The most northern of the halls at the heart of the *Forbidden City*, and home of *Ming* empresses.

Palace of Heavenly Purity
The largest of the three halls at the heart of the *Forbidden City*, where the *emperor* met visitors and advisors.

Jesuit priests

Palace Museum
The name given to the *Forbidden City* after China's *communist revolution*.

pavilion
A grand building, often with a tent-shaped roof.

peasant
Poor workers from the countryside who do not own the land they farm.

Peking Man
The name given to *Homo erectus* remains found in a cave near *Beijing* (or Peking) in 1923–27.

People's Republic of China
The full, modern name for the country of China since *communist* rule began in 1949.

Polo, Marco (1254–1324)
A traveller from the Italian port of Venice, who wrote a famous description of the 17 years he spent in China.

A vase from the Ming period

Prince Gong (1833–98)

The half-brother of the *Qing emperor Xianfeng*. Prince Gong stayed in *Beijing* in 1860 as European troops attacked the city, later making a deal with the invaders.

Puyi (1906–67)

China's last *emperor*, twelfth of the *Qing dynasty*.

Qing

The last *dynasty* to rule China, from 1644 to 1911.

Red Guards

The *revolutionary* student group whose violent support for *Mao Zedong* tore apart Chinese life during the *Cultural Revolution*.

Red Turbans

A *peasant* army that led the rebellion against China's *Mongol* rulers. The Red Turbans captured *Dadu* in 1368.

revolution

A violent protest in which the people of a country kick out their rulers and govern themselves.

scaffolding

A temporary framework on which workers can stand while constructing a building.

sedan chair

See *litter*

siege

The surrounding of a city in warfare, to stop supplies from reaching it, so that the starving defenders are forced to surrender.

sighting board

A simple instrument used in measuring land.

Summer Palaces

A group of palaces on the borders of *Beijing*, where *emperors* spent the summer months.

surveyor

Someone who measures land.

tapestry

A costly decorative pattern or picture created by weaving.

Emperor Chenghua's attendants carry lanterns on his birthday.

Tiananmen

The main entrance to the *Forbidden City*, in the middle of the south wall. Its name means 'gate of heavenly peace'.

Tongzhi (1856–75)

The ninth *emperor* of the *Qing dynasty*, Tongzhi was controlled and made prisoner by his mother, *Cixi*.

trebuchet

A war machine, or 'siege engine', used for hurling missiles during a *siege*.

venison

The meat of deer.

Xianfeng (1831–61)

The eighth *Qing emperor*, who fled when European troops captured the *Forbidden City* in 1860.

Yan

The *dynasty* that briefly ruled the region where *Beijing* now stands in the 4th century BCE.

Yuan

The *dynasty* started by the *Mongol* people, who in 1215 captured the region where *Beijing* now stands.

Zhengde (1491–1521)

The tenth *emperor* of the *Ming dynasty*, Zhengde was famous for his idleness and love of luxury.

Zhongdu

The name, meaning 'central capital', that the *Jurchen Jin dynasty* gave to the city they built, close to where *Beijing* now stands.

Zhu Yuanzhang (1328–98)

Leader of the *Red Turban* rebels, who became the first *Ming emperor*.

The home of a Yan nobleman

Index

Eunuchs struggle to rescue precious items from the flames during a fire in the Forbidden City in 1514.

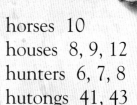

A eunuch falls asleep while supervizing one of emperor Puyi's lessons, in 1919.

Tourists explore the Palace Museum in modern-day Beijing.

'Boxer' troops march into the foreign legation district in 1900.

An armoured vehicle from the 1920s

Rebel soldiers celebrate as China's last emperor, Puyi, is driven away from the Forbidden City in 1924.

Look out for
Through Time:
LONDON
by Richard Platt
in 2009

For Isabella

KINGFISHER

First published 2008 by Kingfisher
an imprint of Macmillan Children's Books
a division of Macmillan Publishers Limited
20 New Wharf Road, London N1 9RR
Basingstoke and Oxford
Associated companies throughout the world
www.panmacmillan.com

Consultant: Dr Kevin McLoughlin, Deputy Curator
of University Museums, University of Durham

Additional illustration work by Monica Favilli and Cecilia Scutti

ISBN 978-0-7534-1576-4

1 3 5 7 9 8 6 4 2
1TR/0208/SHE/CLSN(CLSN)/158MA/C

A CIP catalogue record for this book is available from the British Library.

Printed in Taiwan